Team Spirit®

THE DETROIT RED WINGS

BY

MARK STEWART

Content Consultant
Denis Gibbons
Society for International Hockey Research

NORWOOD HOUSE PRESS

CHICAGO, ILLINOIS

Norwood House Press
P.O. Box 316598
Chicago, Illinois 60631

For information regarding Norwood House Press, please visit our website at:
www.norwoodhousepress.com or call 866-565-2900.

PHOTO CREDITS:
All photos courtesy Getty Images except the following:
Black Book Partners (6, 43), Sport Revue (7), Topps, Inc. (9, 21, 22, 34, 35),
Esso/Imperial Oil Ltd. (14), Associated Press (17), Author's Collection (23, 38),
Parkhurst Products (30), The Hockey News (35 top right),
Bee Hive Golden Corn Syrup/Cargill, Inc. (36), O-Pee-Chee Ltd. (40 top),
Publication Merlin (40 bottom), McDiarmid/Cartophilium (41 top),
Complete Sports Publications, Inc. (41 bottom).
Cover photo: Bruce Bennett/Getty Images
Special thanks to Topps, Inc.

Editor: Mike Kennedy
Designer: Ron Jaffe
Project Management: Black Book Partners, LLC.
Research: Joshua Zaffos
Special thanks to Denise Albrecht and Scott Opperthauser

LIBRARY OF CONGRESS CATALOGING-IN-PUBLICATION DATA

Stewart, Mark, 1960-
  The Detroit Red Wings / by Mark Stewart.
    p. cm. -- (Team spirit)
  Includes bibliographical references and index.
  Summary: "Presents the history and accomplishments of the Detroit Red
Wings hockey team. Includes highlights of players, coaches, and awards,
quotes, timeline, maps, glossary, and websites"--Provided by publisher.
  ISBN-13: 978-1-59953-401-5 (library edition : alk. paper)
  ISBN-10: 1-59953-401-0 (library edition : alk. paper)
  1. Detroit Red Wings (Hockey team)--History--Juvenile literature. I.
Title.
  GV848.D47S74 2010
  796.962'640977434--dc22
                                        2010011632

Manufactured in the United States of America in North Mankato, Minnesota.
159N—072010

COVER PHOTO: Nicklas Lidstrom leads the celebration after Detroit's 2008 Stanley Cup.

Table of Contents

SPORTS WORDS & VOCABULARY WORDS: In this book, you will find many words that are new to you. You may also see familiar words used in new ways. The glossary on page 46 gives the meanings of hockey words, as well as "everyday" words that have special hockey meanings. These words appear in **bold type** throughout the book. The glossary on page 47 gives the meanings of vocabulary words that are not related to hockey. They appear in ***bold italic type*** throughout the book.

Meet the Red Wings

There are many ways to measure success in hockey. You can count the number of goals a team scores. You can wait until the end of the season and see where a team finishes in the **standings**. You can add up the number of awards won by players on the team. Fans of the Detroit Red Wings look at only one thing—championships.

At the end of each season, the **Stanley Cup** is given to the champion of the **National Hockey League (NHL)**. It is a gleaming cup that sits atop many silver bands. Each band has the names of the members of each winning team. The Red Wings have won more Stanley Cups than any other team in the United States.

This book tells the story of the Red Wings. During the team's proud history, Detroit fans have cheered for *legendary* scorers and speedy skaters. They have welcomed stars from all over the world. And they have seen the Red Wings win the Stanley Cup—again and again and again.

Nicklas Lidstrom, Henrik Zetterberg, and Brian Rafalski celebrate a goal during the 2009–10 season.

Way Back When

During the 1920s, the NHL decided to expand from Canada into the U.S. The league chose Detroit, Michigan as one of its new cities. At the same time, the Victoria Cougars were struggling, even though they had captured the Stanley Cup in 1925. Their owners in

Detroit saw an opportunity. They brought the Cougars from Western Canada to Michigan.

The Detroit Cougars played their first NHL season in 1926–27. One year later, they hired Jack Adams to help run the team. He would work for the club for the next 36 years. Among other things, Adams helped rename Detroit's club. After four seasons as the Cougars, the team changed its name to the Falcons.

In 1932, a businessman named James Norris bought the club. He wanted to put his own stamp on the team. Norris picked the name Red Wings and told Adams to build a winner.

The "Wings" reached the **Stanley Cup Finals** for the first time in 1933–34. Over the next 32 seasons, they would play for the NHL championship 17 more times and win the Stanley

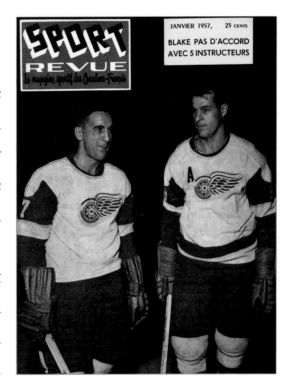

Cup seven times. The leaders of the Red Wings during the 1930s included Herbie Lewis, Larry Aurie, and Marty Barry. Detroit's top player was Ebbie Goodfellow, a defenseman who skated and shot like a forward.

A new group of stars came to Detroit in the 1940s, including Sid Abel, Ted Lindsay, and Gordie Howe. They played together on the high-scoring "Production Line." The Red Wings won four Stanley Cups in the early 1950s. Their stars included center Alex Delvecchio, defensemen Red Kelly and Leo Reise Jr., and goalie Terry Sawchuk.

By the 1960s, only Howe, Delvecchio, and Sawchuk remained from these great clubs. They formed the heart of a fantastic new squad. From 1961 to 1966, Detroit made it to the Stanley Cup Finals four times. Unfortunately, the Red Wings fell short each time, despite the contributions of **hard-nosed** players such as Norm Ullman, Bill Gadsby, Marcel Pronovost, and Roger Crozier.

In the 1970s and 1980s, the Red Wings struggled for the first time in team history. They had some bad luck, but they also made some

LEFT: Jack Adams, one of the team's pioneers. **ABOVE**: Ted Lindsay and Gordie Howe pose for the cover of a 1957 magazine.

poor decisions. Mickey Redmond was an amazing scorer, but he hurt his back. Marcel Dionne set a record for most points by a **rookie**, but he was traded away. Reed Larson, a defenseman with a great slapshot, was also traded. John Ogrodnick was one of the top left wings in the NHL, but the team failed to surround him with good players.

Sergei Fedorov · center
DETROIT RED WINGS®

Detroit's luck began to change after it **drafted** Steve Yzerman in 1983. In the 1990s, Yzerman became the leader of a powerhouse team. At the time, many hockey stars from Russia were coming to the NHL. The Red Wings added Slava Fetisov, Slava Kozlov, Igor Larionov, Vladimir Konstantinov, and Sergei Fedorov. Few were better than Fedorov. He had a very hard slapshot and seemed to be everywhere on the ice at once.

The Wings added even more talented stars and **veterans** over the next few years, including goalie Mike Vernon and defensemen Nicklas Lidstrom and Larry Murphy. In 1996–97, Detroit won the Stanley Cup for the first time in 42 seasons. In 1997–98, the Wings won it again. Lidstrom, Yzerman, Fedorov, and Larionov were still around four years later when Detroit won the Stanley Cup for the 10th time.

LEFT: Steve Yzerman looks to pass the puck to a teammate.
ABOVE: A trading card of Russian star Sergei Fedorov—he teamed with Yzerman to bring the Stanley Cup back to Detroit.

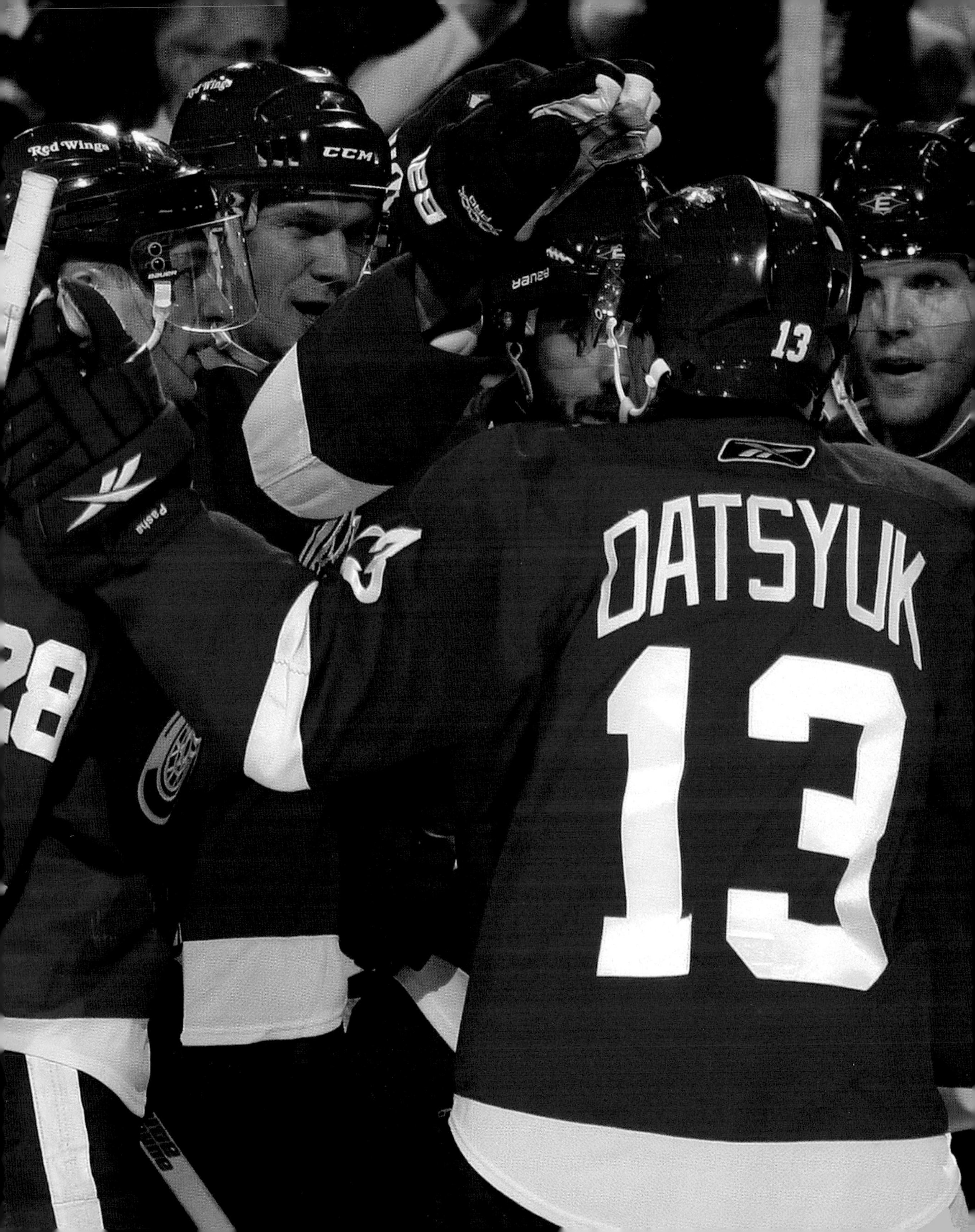
Red Wings
CCM
DATSYUK
13

The Team Today

The Red Wings showed how a team of *experienced*, unselfish players could come together and win the Stanley Cup. In the years after the club's 2001–02 championship, however, many of those older players left the team or retired. So did Scotty Bowman, who coached Detroit to three NHL titles. Could the Red Wings win with a new coach and young players?

The team built its **roster** around Nicklas Lidstrom, its superstar defenseman. The Wings also brought back two of their Stanley Cup-winning goalies, Chris Osgood and Dominik Hasek, and traded for a few players with experience in the **playoffs**. But the future was in the hands of exciting, young stars such as Pavel Datsyuk, Henrik Zetterberg, Johan Franzen, Niklas Kronwall, Jiri Hudler, and Jimmy Howard.

In 2007–08, the Red Wings led the NHL with 54 victories. Coach Mike Babcock guided them through the playoffs and into the Stanley Cup Finals. Detroit defeated the Pittsburgh Penguins to win the 11th championship in team history.

The Wings congratulate Pavel Datsyuk after a goal during the 2009–10 season.

Home Ice

During Detroit's first season in the NHL, the team played in another country. The Cougars used an arena across the river in Windsor, Ontario, Canada while waiting for workers to finish construction on their new arena, the Olympia, in Detroit. Fans loved the Olympia. They called it the "Big Old Red Barn." The Red Wings played there for more than five **decades**.

Two days after Christmas in 1979, the Wings moved into a new home, Joe Louis Arena. Six weeks later, the NHL played its **All-Star Game** at "The Joe." The fans stood and cheered for almost 10 minutes when former Detroit star Gordie Howe was introduced. He was playing in his final NHL season as a member of the Hartford Whalers.

BY THE NUMBERS

- *The team's arena has 20,066 seats for hockey.*
- *The arena cost $57 million to build in the 1970s.*
- *In 2010, the team announced a plan to build a new hockey arena in the future.*

The Red Wings skate against the Dallas Stars at "The Joe" during the 2007–08 playoffs.

Dressed for Success

The Red Wings got their name in 1932 from their new owner, James Norris. He also designed the team's *logo*, which features a "flying" wheel. Norris got the idea from an old hockey team called the Winged Wheelers. He hoped the new logo would draw new fans to the Wings. Back then, thousands upon thousands of people in Michigan built cars for a living. The flying wheel reminded them of the pride they had in their industry.

Detroit's colors have been red and white since the team's first season. The Red Wings usually wear red sweaters for home games and white ones for games on the road. From time to time, the team wears a third, old-style uniform. It is reserved for special games only. The players wear red pants for all games.

Norm ULLMAN

Norm Ullman models Detroit's road uniform from the 1960s.

UNIFORM BASICS

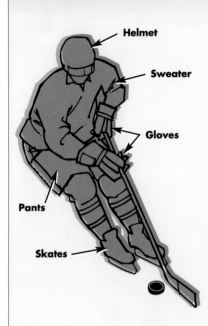

Helmet

Sweater

Gloves

Pants

Skates

The hockey uniform has five important parts:

- Helmet
- Sweater
- Pants
- Gloves
- Skates

Hockey helmets are made of hard plastic with softer padding inside. Some players also wear visors to protect their eyes.

The hockey uniform top is called a sweater. Players wear padding underneath it to protect their shoulders, spine and ribs. Padded hockey pants, or "breezers," extend from the waist to the knees. Players also wear padding on their knees and shins.

Hockey gloves protect the top of the hand and the wrist. Only a thin layer of leather covers the palm, which helps a player control his stick. A goalie wears two different gloves—one for catching pucks and one for blocking them. Goalies also wear heavy leg pads and a mask. They paint their masks to match their personalities and team colors.

All players wear hockey skates. The blade is curved at each end. The skate top is made from metal, plastic, nylon, and either real or **synthetic** leather. Goalies wear skates that have extra protection on the toe and ankle.

Jimmy Howard wears the team's 2009–10 road uniform.

We Won!

The Red Wings won their first Stanley Cup in 1935–36. Goalie Norm Smith led them to victory over the Toronto Maple Leafs. One year later, they played the New York Rangers in the Stanley Cup Finals. Smith was injured, but Earl Robertson came through in his place. Detroit became the first U.S. team to win two Stanley Cups in a row.

The Wings returned to the Stanley Cup Finals six times during the 1940s, but they won the championship just once. After losing in the finals in 1940–41 and 1941–42, the Wings returned in 1942–43. They faced the Boston Bruins. This time, Detroit swept Boston in four games. Mud Bruneteau and Don Grosso each scored a **hat trick** in the series, and goalie Johnny Mowers **shut out** the Bruins in the final two games.

The 1949–50 season was an amazing one for the Red Wings. By this time, the line of Ted Lindsay, Sid Abel, and Gordie Howe was being called the best trio ever. They finished 1–2–3 in the NHL scoring race.

The Rangers were not impressed. They battled Detroit in the finals to a thrilling seventh game. In the second **overtime**, George Gee of the

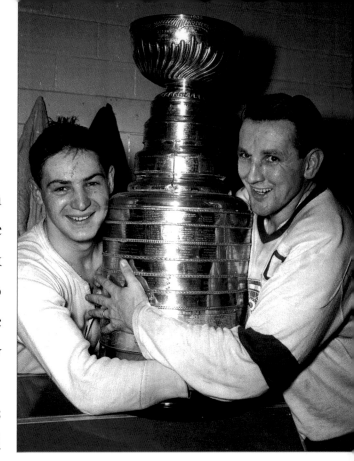

Terry Sawchuk and Sid Abel hug the Stanley Cup after Detroit's championship in 1951–52.

Red Wings slipped a pass from behind the net to teammate Pete Babando. He whacked the puck through a forest of players and into the goal for a 4–3 victory. It was the first time a Game 7 of the Stanley Cup Finals was won in overtime.

Two years later, the Red Wings had a hot young goalie named Terry Sawchuk. He backed up a great defense led by Red Kelly. Detroit finished the season with the league's best record, and then swept through the playoffs without losing a game. In the Stanley Cup Finals, they rolled over the Montreal Canadiens in four games. Some fans say this was the best Detroit team ever.

The Red Wings won the Stanley Cup again in 1953–54. This time they needed seven games to beat the Canadiens. The last game went into overtime. Detroit won on a surprising play. Tony Leswick flipped the puck toward the Montreal goal, and it found its way into the net after bouncing off a defenseman. A year later, the Wings and

Canadiens met again for the championship. Again the series lasted seven games. Detroit won with strong goaltending from Sawchuk and excellent offense by Howe and Alex Delvecchio. Howe's 12 points in the finals set a record.

Detroit fans believed there would be many more Stanley Cups in the team's future. But no one imagined it would take 42 years to win the next one. In 1996–97, the Red Wings put together a team of modern stars that liked to play old-time hockey. Steve Yzerman, Sergei Fedorov, and Brendan Shanahan led Detroit to a sweep of the

Philadelphia Flyers. Mike Vernon was nearly *unbeatable* in the net for the Wings.

One year later, Chris Osgood was Detroit's goalie. He was just as good in the playoffs as Vernon had been the year before. The Red Wings swept the Washington Capitals in four games to claim their ninth Stanley Cup.

The Wings won the Cup again in 2001–02. Yzerman, Fedorov, and Shanahan were joined by four more "old-timers"—Brett Hull, Dominik Hasek, Chris Chelios, and Luc Robitaille. Hull scored 10 goals in the playoffs, and Detroit beat the Carolina Hurricanes in the Stanley Cup Finals.

By 2007–08, a new *generation* had taken over for the Red Wings. Young stars Henrik Zetterberg, Pavel Datsyuk, Johan Franzen, and Niklas Kronwall followed the lead of Nicklas Lidstrom—a hero of past championships. Detroit defeated the Pittsburgh Penguins in six games to capture its 11th Stanley Cup.

LEFT: Larry Murphy and Nicklas Lidstrom come to the aid of Mike Vernon after a shot by the Philadelphia Flyers.   **ABOVE**: Chris Chelios and Henrik Zetterberg celebrate Detroit's 11th Stanley Cup.

Go-To Guys

To be a true star in the NHL, you need more than a great slapshot. You have to be a "go-to guy"—someone teammates trust to make the winning play when the seconds are ticking away in a big game. Red Wings fans have had a lot to cheer about over the years, including these great stars …

THE PIONEERS

EBBIE GOODFELLOW   Center/Defenseman

• BORN: 4/9/1906 • DIED: 9/10/1965 • PLAYED FOR TEAM: 1929–30 TO 1942–43

When Ebbie Goodfellow joined Detroit, he was a high-scoring center. Later, coach Jack Adams made him a defenseman. Goodfellow led the Red Wings to the Stanley Cup two seasons in a row and won the Hart Trophy in 1939–40 as the NHL's **Most Valuable Player (MVP)**.

SID ABEL   Center

• BORN: 2/22/1918 • DIED: 2/8/2000 • PLAYED FOR TEAM: 1938–39 TO 1951–52

Sid Abel was named team captain at age 24. He was an **All-Star** as a left wing and then as a center. Abel was the leader of Detroit's "Production Line." He won the Hart Trophy in 1948–49.

TED LINDSAY   Left Wing

- BORN: 7/29/1925 • PLAYED FOR TEAM: 1944–45 TO 1956–57 & 1964–65

Ted Lindsay stood only 5′ 8″ and weighed just 160 pounds, but he was pure muscle and energy. His nickname was "Terrible Ted." He won the **Art Ross Trophy** in 1949–50.

GORDIE HOWE   Right Wing

- BORN: 3/31/1928 • PLAYED FOR TEAM: 1946–47 TO 1970–71

Gordie Howe was almost impossible to stop. He had a hard, accurate shot, and no one was better at protecting the puck. When Howe left the Wings, he was the NHL's all-time leader with 786 goals.

RED KELLY   Defenseman

- BORN: 7/9/1927
- PLAYED FOR TEAM: 1947–48 TO 1959–60

Red Kelly

Like Ebbie Goodfellow, Red Kelly was a fantastic **two-way player**. He was the best scoring defenseman of his *era*. Kelly won the Lady Byng Memorial Trophy for good sportsmanship three times with Detroit.

TERRY SAWCHUK   Goalie

- BORN: 12/28/1929 • DIED: 5/31/1970
- PLAYED FOR TEAM: 1949–50 TO 1954–55, 1957–58 TO 1963–64 & 1968–69

Terry Sawchuk was the best young goalie anyone had ever seen. In fact, Detroit traded star Harry Lumley to give Sawchuk more playing time. He rewarded the Wings with 56 shutouts over the next five seasons.

ALEX DELVECCHIO   Center

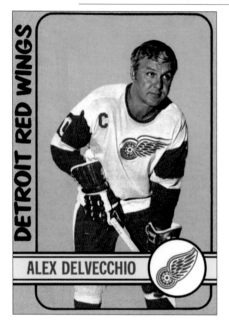

DETROIT RED WINGS

ALEX DELVECCHIO

- BORN: 12/4/1931
- PLAYED FOR TEAM: 1950–51 TO 1973–74

Alex Delvecchio replaced Sid Abel on the "Production Line." His quick skating and *precision* passing made him a star in Detroit for more than 20 seasons. No one in history played more games for the same team than Delvecchio.

STEVE YZERMAN   Center

- BORN: 5/9/1965
- PLAYED FOR TEAM: 1983–84 TO 2005–06

Red Wings fans had gone nearly three decades without a Stanley Cup before Steve Yzerman arrived in Detroit. He would lead the team to three championships. On the way, Yzerman had one of the greatest seasons in history, with 65 goals and 90 **assists** in 1988–89.

SERGEI FEDOROV   Center

- BORN: 12/13/1969 • PLAYED FOR TEAM: 1990–91 TO 2002–03

After leaving Russia to play in the NHL, Sergei Fedorov quickly proved he was among the best centers in the league. He won the NHL's fastest skater and hardest shot contests, and was also named winner of the Hart Trophy in 1993–94.

NICKLAS LIDSTROM — Defenseman

- BORN: 4/28/1970
- FIRST SEASON WITH TEAM: 1991–92

Nicklas Lidstrom won the **Norris Trophy** six times. He led the Red Wings to four championships from 1996–97 to 2007–08. Few players have ever "read" the ice as well as Lidstrom. He could see a play developing and stop it with a check or by stealing the puck.

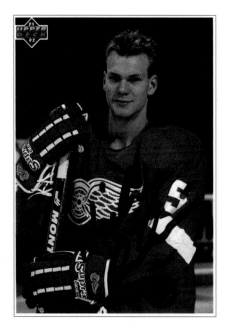

PAVEL DATSYUK — Center

- BORN: 7/20/1978 • FIRST SEASON WITH TEAM: 2001–02

From the moment Pavel Datsyuk joined the Red Wings, Detroit fans knew he was something special. He seemed to know exactly when and where to pass the puck to give his teammates a great chance to score.

HENRIK ZETTERBERG — Center/Left Wing

- BORN: 10/9/1980 • FIRST SEASON WITH TEAM: 2002–03

Henrik Zetterberg was a smooth skater and a talented scorer. He made the game look easy. Zetterberg scored the goal that won the 2007–08 Stanley Cup—and then signed the biggest contract in team history!

LEFT: Alex Delvecchio
ABOVE: A signed trading card of Nicklas Lidstrom.

Behind the Bench

The first coach to lead the Red Wings to the Stanley Cup was Jack Adams. He was behind the bench for more than 900 games. Today, the NHL's top coach receives the Jack Adams Award. Three Detroit coaches have won that award—Bobby Kromm, Jacques Demers, and Scotty Bowman.

Bowman was behind the bench for Detroit's championships in 1996–97, 1997–98, and 2001–02. Tommy Ivan, Jimmy Skinner, and Mike Babcock also led the Wings to the Stanley Cup. Ivan took over from Adams in 1947. The team won three Stanley Cups under Ivan. Skinner followed him and won the Cup in 1954–55. Babcock led the team to victory in 2007–08.

Since 1982, the Red Wings have been owned by Mike Illitch. From the day Illitch took control, he and his relatives treated everyone in the *organization* like they were part of their family. That includes Ken Holland, who joined the Red Wings as an executive in the 1980s. He helped build the Stanley Cup champs of the 1990s and 2000s.

Scotty Bowman and Mike Babcock, two of the coaches who led the Red Wings to the Stanley Cup.

One Great Day

One of the hardest things to do in sports is win the Stanley Cup two years in a row. By the 1990s, the Red Wings had already done it twice, in the 1930s and again in the 1950s. Six days after winning the Cup in 1996–97, the team lost an important leader when Vladimir Konstantinov was badly injured in a car accident. He suffered brain damage and would never play again. Slava Fetisov was in the same crash. Luckily, he escaped unhurt.

All season long, the Wings missed Konstantinov. He had helped create great **team chemistry**. He also had a special talent for knowing exactly what would drive opponents crazy. The Red Wings sewed a special patch onto their sweaters with his initials and the word "Believe." The Wings had the talent to win back-to-back titles. As the 1997–98 playoffs began, the question was: Did they have the heart?

The Red Wings answered this question by beating the Phoenix Coyotes, St. Louis Blues, and then the Dallas Stars. Each series was tough, but Detroit never gave up. By the time the Wings reached the

The Red Wings show the "V" sign as they wheel Vladimir Konstantinov around the ice with the Stanley Cup.

Stanley Cup Finals, they were unstoppable. They swept the Washington Capitals in four games.

Following their victory in Game 4, the Red Wings brought Konstantinov onto the ice in a wheelchair. They gave "Vlady" the Stanley Cup and then pushed him around the rink for a victory lap. He smiled widely and held up two fingers to make a "V" for *Victory*. Most of his teammates had tears in their eyes. Even the Capitals had to admire the moment.

"That's outstanding what they did," said Washington coach Ron Wilson. "You'd only see that in hockey."

Legend Has It

Who was the greatest team captain in hockey?

LEGEND HAS IT that Steve Yzerman was. The Red Wings named him captain in 1986–87, at the age of 21. At first Yzerman led by example. He scored at least 45 goals six years in a row. Later, he became an excellent defensive player, too. In 1996–97 and again in 1997–98, Yzerman led the Red Wings to the Stanley Cup. He retired after 20 years as captain. No one in the history of North American team sports had served longer for one club.

Steve Yzerman wears the captain's "C."

Who was the first player to "hoist" the Stanley Cup?

LEGEND HAS IT that Ted Lindsay was. After Detroit defeated the New York Rangers in double-overtime in Game 7 of the 1950 Stanley Cup Finals, the trophy was handed to team captain Sid Abel. Lindsay grabbed it from Abel and hoisted it high above his head. He skated slowly around the rink, so all the fans could get a good look at it. Hoisting the Cup has been a hockey *tradition* ever since.

Which Red Wing made more money in one season than an entire team?

LEGEND HAS IT that Sergei Fedorov did. In 1997–98, the Red Wings signed Fedorov to a new contract, which included a $14 million bonus. The following season, the Nashville Predators paid all of their players a total of $13.6 million. It was hard to argue that Fedorov was overpaid. Once, he scored all five goals in a 5–4 victory for the Wings.

It Really Happened

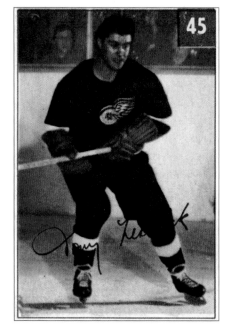

During the early 1950s, Red Wings fans loved to talk about how their team won the 1950 Stanley Cup with an overtime goal in Game 7 of the finals. It had never happened before, and most doubted that it would ever happen again. But as amazing as that moment was, it was nothing compared to the crazy finish of the 1954 Stanley Cup.

Once again, the Red Wings were locked in a fierce battle for the championship, this time with the Montreal Canadiens. The series was tied at three games apiece, and Game 7 in Detroit was knotted 1–1 after three periods. For the second time in five years, the NHL crown would go to the first team that scored in overtime.

The overtime period was just a few minutes old when Tony Leswick decided to flip the puck into the Montreal end. The Red Wings were about to make a **line change**. Leswick headed to the bench.

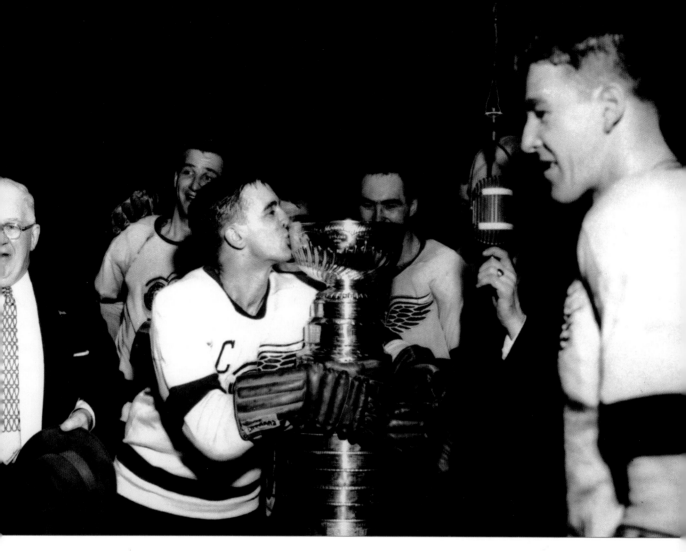

Suddenly the Olympia exploded in cheers. Leswick looked back to see the red goal light flashing. His teammates were leaping over the boards to celebrate. Leswick was **stunned**. Doug Harvey, Montreal's top defenseman, had tried to knock the puck down with his glove. Instead, he tipped it into his own net. Leswick had scored the game-winning goal, and he was the only one who had not seen it!

LEFT: Tony Leswick, the hero for the Red Wings in 1953–54.
ABOVE: Ted Lindsay kisses the Cup as Jack Adams and his players celebrate around him.

Team Spirit

Detroit is known as "Hockeytown." The name fits the city perfectly. Thousands of fans pour into the Red Wings' arena for every game. Just as many players skate for **amateur** and **minor-league** teams all over the state. In fact, the first **professional** hockey clubs played in Michigan. The NHL was born in Canada more than 10 years later.

Not surpisingly, the Red Wings have plenty of traditions. The most famous is octopus-throwing! It started in 1952, when two brothers brought an octopus to Detroit's arena and threw it on the ice. At the time, only four teams made the playoffs. It took eight wins to capture the Stanley Cup. An octopus has eight arms. The Wings won eight games in a row, and fans have been throwing the eight-armed creatures ever since.

Fans who don't have time to stop by the seafood shop can still enjoy Al the Octopus. Al is the team's giant purple *mascot*. He is named after Al Sobotka, the man who cleans up the ice after Detroit fans throw octopuses on it. Sobotka also drives the machine that cleans the ice between periods. Al the Octopus lives in the rafters of Detroit's arena. He is raised up there before every playoff game.

Al the Octopus is lowered to the ice in Detroit's arena before a 2008–09 playoff game.

Timeline

The hockey season is played from October through June. That means each season takes place at the end of one year and the beginning of the next. In this timeline, the accomplishments of the Red Wings are shown by season.

1926–27
The team joins the NHL as the Detroit Cougars.

1951–52
The team goes unbeaten in the playoffs to win the Stanley Cup.

1932–33
James Norris buys the team and changes its name to the Red Wings.

1942–43
Johnny Mowers wins the **Vezina Trophy**.

1962–63
Gordie Howe wins his sixth scoring title.

Gordie Howe

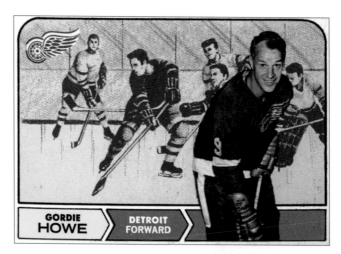

GORDIE HOWE   DETROIT FORWARD

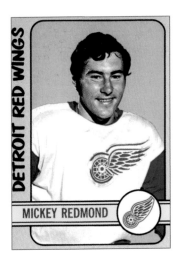

Mickey Redmond

Henrik Zetterberg, a leader on the 2007–08 team.

1972–73
Mickey Redmond is the first Red Wing to score 50 goals in a season.

2007–08
The Wings win their 11th Stanley Cup.

1986–87
Steve Yzerman is named team captain at age 21.

1996–97
Detroit wins its first Stanley Cup in 42 years.

2001–02
Dominik Hasek sets an NHL record with six shutouts in the playoffs.

Dominik Hasek makes a save during the 2002 playoffs.

Fun Facts

PASSING GRADE

In the 2001–02 playoffs, Dominik Hasek did something no goalie had ever done. The Red Wings and Colorado Avalanche were tied in overtime. Hasek fired a pass to Steve Yzerman, who fed the puck to Fredrik Olausson. Olausson scored to win the game. Hasek got an assist—the first ever for a goalie in an overtime playoff game.

Terry Sawchuck

ZERO HEROES

Terry Sawchuk had 11 shutouts as a rookie for the Red Wings in 1950–51. Many fans thought no one would ever approach this record. They were wrong. In 1955–56, Glen Hall had 12 shutouts in his first season in Detroit.

FATHER FIGURE

The first time Gordie Howe played in a Detroit game in front of his dad was on "Gordie Howe Night" in 1959. Howe received a car from the team—and his dad was sitting in it!

SWEDE VICTORY

In 2005–06, Detroit often played Nicklas Lidstrom, Henrik Zetterberg, Tomas Holmstrom, Niklas Kronwall, and Mikael Samuelsson at the same time. The "Swedish Five" also played together for their country in the 2006 *Olympics*—and led Sweden to a gold medal!

BANG FOR THE BUCK

During the 1980s, Detroit had two of the roughest players ever to take the ice. Right wings Bob Probert and Joey Kocur—who played the same position on different lines—were known as the "Bruise Brothers."

ROGER AND OUT

The Red Wings lost the 1966 Stanley Cup Finals, but Roger Crozier was so spectacular in goal that he won the Conn Smythe Trophy as MVP of the playoffs.

LEFT: Terry Sawchuk
ABOVE: Henrik Zetterberg, Tomas Holmstrom, and Mikael Samuelsson celebrate a goal during the 2006 Olympics.

Talking Hockey

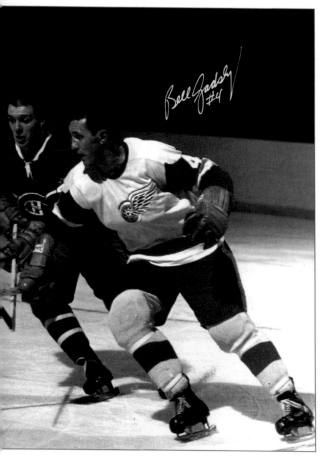

"You've got to love what you're doing. If you love it, you can overcome any **handicap** or the soreness or all the aches and pains, and continue to play for a long, long time."

— *Gordie Howe, on what it takes to last in the NHL*

"Gordie Howe wasn't just the best hockey player I've ever seen, but the greatest athlete."

— *Bill Gadsby, on his goal-scoring teammate*

"If you play well and win, you're a heck of a leader … if you don't play well and don't win, you're a lousy leader."

— *Steve Yzerman, on winning, losing, and leadership in hockey*

ABOVE: An autographed photo of Bill Gadsby.
RIGHT: Igor Larionov

"I've been playing professional hockey for twenty years and this is the happiest moment of my life."
—*Igor Larionov, on Detroit's 1996–97 Stanley Cup victory*

"When he's hot, it's so much fun to play with him because he can do so much on the ice. If you just keep your stick down, you know you're going to get the puck. You don't really know how he does it."
—*Tomas Holmstrom, on the passing skill of Pavel Datsyuk*

"For my game, I don't need to score the goal. I need someone to start thinking about me and forgetting about scoring goals."
—*Vladimir Konstantinov, on the value of being a pest on the ice*

"In this game, you have to be mean or you're going to get pushed around. I keep telling myself to be mean! Be mean!"
—*Ted Lindsay, on how a small player survives in the NHL*

For the Record

T he great Red Wings teams and players have left their marks on the record books. These are the "best of the best" …

Ebbie Goodfellow

Gordie Howe

RED WINGS AWARD WINNERS

ART ROSS TROPHY
TOP SCORER

Ted Lindsay	1949–50
Gordie Howe	1950–51
Gordie Howe	1951–52
Gordie Howe	1952–53
Gordie Howe	1953–54
Gordie Howe	1956–57
Gordie Howe	1962–63

HART MEMORIAL TROPHY
MOST VALUABLE PLAYER

Ebbie Goodfellow	1939–40
Sid Abel	1948–49
Gordie Howe	1951–52
Gordie Howe	1952–53
Gordie Howe	1956–57
Gordie Howe	1957–58
Gordie Howe	1959–60
Gordie Howe	1962–63
Sergei Fedorov	1993–94

VEZINA TROPHY
TOP GOALTENDER

Norm Smith	1936–37
Johnny Mowers	1942–43
Terry Sawchuk	1951–52
Terry Sawchuk	1952–53
Terry Sawchuk	1954–55

CONN SMYTHE TROPHY
MVP DURING PLAYOFFS

Roger Crozier	1965–66
Mike Vernon	1996–97
Steve Yzerman	1997–98
Nicklas Lidstrom	2001–02
Henrik Zetterberg	2007–08

CALDER TROPHY
TOP ROOKIE

Carl Voss	1932–33
Jim McFadden	1947–48
Terry Sawchuk	1950–51
Glenn Hall	1955–56
Roger Crozier	1964–65

JAMES NORRIS MEMORIAL TROPHY
TOP DEFENSIVE PLAYER

Red Kelly	1953–54
Paul Coffey	1994–95
Nicklas Lidstrom	2000–01
Nicklas Lidstrom	2001–02
Nicklas Lidstrom	2002–03
Nicklas Lidstrom	2005–06
Nicklas Lidstrom	2006–07
Nicklas Lidstrom	2007–08

RED WINGS ACHIEVEMENTS

ACHIEVEMENT	YEAR
Stanley Cup Finalists	1933–34
Stanley Cup Champions	1935–36
Stanley Cup Champions	1936–37
Stanley Cup Finalists	1940–41
Stanley Cup Finalists	1941–42
Stanley Cup Champions	1942–43
Stanley Cup Finalists	1944–45
Stanley Cup Finalists	1947–48
Stanley Cup Finalists	1948–49
Stanley Cup Champions	1949–50
Stanley Cup Champions	1951–52
Stanley Cup Champions	1953–54
Stanley Cup Champions	1954–55
Stanley Cup Finalists	1955–56
Stanley Cup Finalists	1960–61
Stanley Cup Finalists	1962–63
Stanley Cup Finalists	1963–64
Stanley Cup Finalists	1965–66
Stanley Cup Finalists	1994–95
Stanley Cup Champions	1996–97
Stanley Cup Champions	1997–98
Stanley Cup Champions	2001–02
Stanley Cup Champions	2007–08
Stanley Cup Finalists	2008–09

ROGER CROZIER
NHL Rookie Of The Year

TOP: Sid Abel, who helped the Wings win three Stanley Cups.
BOTTOM: Roger Crozier, the NHL's top rookie in 1964–65.

Pinpoints

The history of a hockey team is made up of many smaller stories. These stories take place all over the map—not just in the city a team calls "home." Match the pushpins on these maps to the Team Facts and you will begin to see the story of the Red Wings unfold!

TEAM FACTS

1   Detroit, Michigan—*The team has played here since 1926–27.*

2   Chicago, Illinois—*Chris Chelios was born here.*

3   Minneapolis, Minnesota—*Reed Larson was born here.*

4   Kirkland Lake, Ontario, Canada—*Mickey Redmond was born here.*

5   Winnipeg, Manitoba, Canada—*Terry Sawchuk was born here.*

6   Calgary, Alberta, Canada—*Mike Vernon was born here.*

7   Melville, Saskatchewan, Canada—*Sid Abel was born here.*

Sergei Fedorov

8   Cranbrook, British Columbia, Canada—*Steve Yzerman was born here.*

9   Belfast, Northern Ireland—*Jim McFadden was born here.*

10 Njurunda, Sweden—*Henrik Zetterberg was born here.*

11 Pardubice, Czechoslovakia*—*Dominik Hasek was born here.*

12 Pskov, Russia—*Sergei Fedorov was born here.*

* Now known as the Czech Republic.

Faceoff

Hockey is played between two teams of six skaters. Each team has a goalie, two defensemen, and a forward line that includes a left wing, right wing and center. The goalie's job is to stop the puck from crossing the red goal line. A hockey goal is six feet wide and four feet high. The hockey puck is a round disk made of hard rubber. It weighs approximately six ounces.

During a game, players skate as hard as they can for a full "shift." When they get tired, they take a seat on the bench, and a new group jumps off the bench and over the boards to take their place. Forwards play together in set groups, or "lines," and defensemen do too.

There are rules that prevent players from injuring or interfering with opponents. However, players are allowed to bump, or "check," each other when they battle for the puck. Because hockey is a fast game played by strong athletes, sometimes checks can be rough!

If a player breaks a rule, a penalty is called by the referee. For most penalties, the player must sit in the penalty box for two minutes. This gives the other team a one-skater advantage, or "power play." The team down a skater is said to be "short-handed."

NHL games have three 20-minute periods—60 minutes in all—and the team that scores the most goals when time has run out is the winner. If the score is tied, the teams play an overtime period. The first team to score during overtime wins. If the game is still tied, then it is decided

44

by a shootout—a one-on-one contest between the goalies and the best shooters. During the Stanley Cup playoffs, no shootouts are held. The teams play until the tie is broken.

Things happen so quickly in hockey that it is easy to overlook set plays. The next time you watch a game, see if you can spot these plays:

 PLAY LIST

DEFLECTION—Sometimes a shooter does not try to score a goal. Instead, he aims his shot so that a teammate can touch the puck with his stick and suddenly change its direction. If the goalie is moving to stop the first shot, he may be unable to adjust to the "deflection."

GIVE-AND-GO—When a skater is closely guarded and cannot get an open shot, he sometimes passes to a teammate with the idea of getting a return pass in better position to shoot. The "give-and-go" works when the defender turns to follow the pass and loses track of his man. By the time he recovers, it is too late.

ONE-TIMER—When a player receives a pass, he must control the puck and position himself for a shot. This gives the defense a chance to react. Some players are skilled enough to shoot the instant a pass arrives for a "one-timer." A well-aimed one-timer is almost impossible to stop.

PULLING THE GOALIE—Sometimes in the final moments of a game, the team that is behind will try a risky play. To gain an extra skater, the team will pull the goalie out of the game and replace him with a center, wing, or defenseman. This gives the team a better chance to score. It also leaves the goal unprotected and allows the opponent to score an "empty-net goal."

Glossary

HOCKEY WORDS TO KNOW

ALL-STAR—An award given to the league's best players at the end of each season.

ALL-STAR GAME—The annual game featuring the NHL's best players. Prior to 1967, the game was played at the beginning of the season between the league champion and an All-Star squad. Today it is played during the season. The game doesn't count in the standings.

AMATEUR—Someone who plays a sport without being paid.

ART ROSS TROPHY—The award given to the league's top scorer each season.

ASSISTS—Passes that lead to a goal.

DRAFTED—Chosen from a group of the best junior hockey, college, and international players. The NHL draft is held each summer.

HAT TRICK—Three goals in one game.

LINE CHANGE—The switching of a group of fresh forwards for a group of tired ones. Line changes usually take place every minute or two.

MINOR-LEAGUE—A level of play below the NHL.

MOST VALUABLE PLAYER (MVP)—The award given each year to the league's best player; also given to the best player in the playoffs and All-Star Game.

NATIONAL HOCKEY LEAGUE (NHL)—The league that began play in 1917–18 and is still in existence today.

NORRIS TROPHY—The award given to the league's top defenseman each season.

OVERTIME—The extra 20-minute period played when a game is tied after 60 minutes. Teams continue playing overtime periods until one team scores a goal and wins.

PLAYOFFS—The games played after the season to determine the league champion.

PROFESSIONAL—A player or team that plays a sport for money.

ROOKIE—A player in his first season.

ROSTER—The list of a team's active players.

SHUT OUT—Hold an opponent scoreless.

STANDINGS—A daily list of teams, starting with the team with the best record and ending with the team with the worst record.

STANLEY CUP—The championship trophy of North American hockey since 1893, and of the NHL since 1927.

STANLEY CUP FINALS—The series that determines the NHL champion each season. It has been a best-of-seven series since 1939.

TEAM CHEMISTRY—The way players work together on and off the ice. Winning teams usually have good chemistry.

TWO-WAY PLAYER—A player who is equally good on offense and defense.

VETERANS—Players with great experience.

VEZINA TROPHY—The award given to the league's top goalie each season.

OTHER WORDS TO KNOW

DECADES—Periods of 10 years; also specific periods, such as the 1950s.

ERA—A period of time in history.

EXPERIENCED—Having great knowledge and skill.

GENERATION—A group of people born during the same period of history.

HANDICAP—An obstacle or physical disability.

HARD-NOSED—Able to meet opposition head-on.

LEGENDARY—Famous

LOGO—A symbol or design that represents a company or team.

MASCOT—An animal or person believed to bring a group good luck.

OLYMPICS—An international sports competition held every four years.

ORGANIZATION—A group of people who work together for the same purpose.

PRECISION—Accuracy or exactness.

STUNNED—Shocked and surprised.

SYNTHETIC—Made in a laboratory, not in nature.

TRADITION—A belief or custom that is handed down from generation to generation.

UNBEATABLE—Impossible to defeat.

Places to Go

ON THE ROAD

DETROIT RED WINGS
19 Steve Yzerman Drive
Detroit, Michigan 48226
(313) 394-7000

THE HOCKEY HALL OF FAME
Brookfield Place
30 Yonge Street
Toronto, Ontario, Canada   M5E 1X8
(416) 360-7765

ON THE WEB

THE NATIONAL HOCKEY LEAGUE   www.nhl.com
  • *Learn more about the National Hockey League*

THE DETROIT RED WINGS   redwings.nhl.com
  • *Learn more about the Red Wings*

THE HOCKEY HALL OF FAME   www.hhof.com
  • *Learn more about hockey's greatest players*

ON THE BOOKSHELF

To learn more about the sport of hockey, look for these books at your library or bookstore:

  • Keltie, Thomas. *Inside Hockey! The Legends, Facts, and Feats that Made the Game.* Toronto, Ontario, Canada: Maple Tree Press, 2008.
  • MacDonald, James. *Hockey Skills: How to Play Like a Pro.* Berkeley Heights, New Jersey: Enslow Elementary, 2009.
  • Stewart, Mark and Kennedy, Mike. *Score! The Action and Artistry of Hockey's Magnificent Moment.* Minneapolis, Minnesota: Lerner Publishing Group, 2010.

Index

PAGE NUMBERS IN **BOLD** REFER TO ILLUSTRATIONS.

The Team

MARK STEWART has written over 200 books for kids—and more than a dozen books on hockey, including a history of the Stanley Cup. Like most young hockey fans in the 1960s, Mark loved Gordie Howe—except when he played against his hometown team, the New York Rangers. As an adult, he met all three members of the Production Line: Howe, Ted Lindsay, and Alex Delvecchio. Their autographed photos are on the wall of his office. Mark comes from a family of writers. His grandfather was Sunday Editor of *The New York Times* and his mother was Articles Editor of *Ladies' Home Journal* and *McCall's*, and also wrote for *Sports Illustrated*. Mark has profiled hundreds of athletes over the last 20 years. He has also written several books about New York and New Jersey. Mark is a graduate of Duke University, with a degree in History. He lives with his daughters and wife Sarah overlooking Sandy Hook, New Jersey.

DENIS GIBBONS is a former newsletter editor of the Toronto-based Society for International Hockey Research (SIHR) and a writer and editor with *The Hockey News*. He was a contributing writer to the publication *Kings of the Ice: A History of World Hockey* and has worked as chief hockey researcher at six Winter Olympics for the ABC, CBS, and NBC television networks. Denis also has worked as a researcher for the FOX Sports Network during the Stanley Cup playoffs. He resides in Burlington, Ontario, Canada with his wife Chris.